Super Secrets to Fix My Credit:

Tips, Tricks, and Secrets to Improve Credit Ratings and Fix Bad Credit Scores

(Bonus Section: Recession Proofing Your Job!)

By Ramon Glyde

Super Secrets to Fix My Credit:

Tips, Tricks, and Secrets to Improve Credit Ratings and Fix Bad Credit Scores

by **Ramon Glyde**

Printed in the United States of America

Copyright © 2010 **Ramon Glyde**

Contents

CHAPTER ONE

Credit - understanding genesis of bad credit.

It's very obvious that we now live in a credit world. There are lots of banking institutions offering different forms of credit from credit card to personal loans. The amount of people with credit cards is rising very fast. Apart from that, lots of people can hardly do without credit.

Because of lack of enough financial education and discipline on the part of most of these consumers they often find themselves in bad credit situations like court judgement, bankruptcy, and loan default which often make it difficult for them to get any credit at all in future. You may now want to ask – what exactly is credit?

Credit means that you are getting a service or cash grant to use for your own purpose. You are often bound with a contract or agreement to repay in future as agreed with lender or service provider. Credit exists in different forms like loan, mortgage, or credit card.

Before you can get credit from any financial institution or lending agency, they will first check your credit history. If you have default on loan before or have bad credit history you will find it almost difficult to get credit any time you apply for it.

However, it's possible for you to improve your credit history or build a new good credit history by repairing your credit, thus re-establishing your credit-worthiness. This process is called credit repair. It's the process in which consumers with unfavorable credit histories attempt to re-establish their credit-worthiness.

Though there are lots of credit repair companies nowadays that promises repairing your credit for you, if you can follow simple guide, it's very possible for you to do it yourself – afterall it's your credit.

If you repair your credit it will make it easy for you to get low interest credit, car or home loans. However, with poor credit rating you may not be able to get loan or be subjected to high interest rates and several other unnecessary conditions. So it's very important that you repair your credit if you have bad credit. You will get lots of tips on how to do this easily in this book.

CHAPTER TWO

Credit rating: - how you are scored.

Getting approval for any type of loan depends on your credit rating. If you have average credit rating, you will find it almost impossible to get approved. It's possible to get good rating or even improve you credit rating. Most companies almost use same rating system and if you are able to know more about it you should be able to have better credit score.

Your age is the first factor which it's almost impossible to do anything about. Yes it's possible to lie, but don't because it will make things more difficult for you in future if the creditor get to know. If you are between 24 to 64 years of age you will get one point. Any age bellow or above that will score you zero point.

If you are married you have chance of adding extra point to your score. If not, you still score zero as most creditors see you as a higher risk. Also if you have no dependant you will score zero. But if you have between one to three you will add to your points. Here is how it works – if you have no dependant creditors believe you can skip town and not pay off your credit.

Creditors will also want to know more about your root. They will want to know where you live. Owning a home with a big fat mortgage or even without mortgage will give you more points. How long you stay in your present or previous residence also adds more points to your score. If you've move so often you will score zero point. However, if you've stayed up to 5 years before moving, you will surely get more point. It shows you are a good risk to them.

Other factors that will add to your point are your years on job (the longer the better), kind of job, your monthly income, present debt status, previous credit history and your saving or checking account.

You credit score is usually rate between 350 and 850. The lower your score the more difficult it will be to get loan. Scoring 800 or above should be goal of every consumer. Bellow is list of short tips on how to achieve 800 credit score or above.

Limit the number of credit card you sign up for at a time. The more card you carry the debt will have to live with. If one card is not enough for you make sure you don't sign up for more that three cards. Also make sure that you don't go out with more than one card in your pocket. That way you will limit your purchases when you are outside.

Make sure that you make your payment on time, if possible before the end of grace period if it's part of the service. Late payment will affect your credit score adversely.

Whenever you want to apply for credit make sure that you don't apply for too much credit often. Credit reporting agency may score you low as it means that you can't live without credit.

Another thing that reporting agency consider in scoring you is outstanding balance on your credit account. If you are the type of consumer that often exceeds their limit you are risking your credit score. So make sure you don't exceed 30-35% of your available credit. It doesn't make sense financially to always spend all your credit at a time.

CHAPTER THREE

Your credits score - how you can improve it.

Your credit score is a very important in any financial transaction that you make or intend making in future. So it's good you know what exactly your score is, understand its meaning and learn how you can improve it if it's not good enough.

If you have ever borrow money or utilized credit before it has a score that reflects how well you handle the credit giving to you in the past. The credit score is determine by amount of credit you have, how much money you owe and whether you made payments on time or not.

Your credit score serves as predictor of how likely you are to repay any credit giving to you to your would be creditor or lender. If you usually make payments on time you will surely have good credit history and it will make it easy for you to get loan from banks or credit unions.

Otherwise, you will find it difficult to get any institution for that matter to trust you. If that's your case – it don't have to be the end of the road. In this article you will learn about what you can do to improve your credit score.

Make sure you pay your bills on time. Failure to do this will have negative impact on your credit score.

Make sure you always meet up with the minimum monthly payment on your card if you can't always pay the balances of your credit card each month.

Make sure that you don't exceed your monthly limit. If you can keep to 50% of your limit or less it's better.

Make sure you do away with account you don't use most especially accounts with high annual fees and high interest rates.

CHAPTER FOUR

Credit report – its effect on your personal credit

Lots of people have been denied loan, credit card or other form of credit because of wrong information the lenders find in their credit report. Before banks or any other financial institution grant your application for loan they will first find out about your credit history from bureau by requesting for your credit report.

Credit report is a compilation of your credit history, past financial transactions and personal information possible. This report is usually compiled by accredited agencies known as credit reporting agency.

Credit reporting agencies are organizations that help credit card companies, loan companies, banks, and departmental stores in the country to ascertain the credit worthiness of their would be clients. They provide these companies information about those who are good credit risk and those who are not.

They receive most information about consumers from loan companies, credit card companies, banks, credit and lending sources. In this report you will their will be information on your occupation, place of employment, residence record, court and arrest records, income status, details on payment of your past and present bills and loans.

Once they have detail information from these sources, they give it to any organizations in need of it when requested. Though they keep on file information concerning you and your credit, they don't make final judgments as to your credit worthiness. The decision is up to the credit card companies or any lender which you are dealing with.

The credit score is used by banks, credit card companies, loan lenders and other financial companies to determine your credit worthiness. As a matter of fact, most lenders often based their charges on information in your credit report. Also, some employers often consider few information in your credit report before they employ you. If you have severe financial problems some will find it difficult to employ you.

Whenever you apply for new credit card, loan or any form of credit from any sources lenders will base their acceptance or rejection of your application on your personal credit report. If your credit report shows you've been reliable in the past, then you will most likely get the credit card or loan you apply for.

However, if you have in one way or the other defaulted on particular account or you were constantly late in making payments, it will likely be impossible for you to get the credit you applied for.

While compiling your report the agency or financial institution that's giving them the information may make mistake and give inaccurate information about your credit. If you did not dispute this error and demand necessary changes, they will leave it in your report. You can imagine the possible effects on your life in future. Because of this, it's very important that you check your report at least once a year

.

In other to be able to check your report for possible inaccurate information you have to request for a copy of your report. You can get a copy of this report from credit bureau because it's your personal credit file and you have absolute right to know what is in it.

You have right to know exact information they are giving out concerning your name and credit worthiness. If the report is not good enough or you can proof to yourself that it's all about your past, you can change it. You can build your new credit worthiness. It's possible.

CHAPTER FIVE

Your personal credit report: - how you can correct errors.

People that compile your personal credit reports are human be like me and you, they can make mistake while compiling your reports from various sources. Thus, requesting for a copy of your report often is very important. It will allow you to know what they compile about you. You will be able to discover unfavorable information, request for corrections before they started spreading non-accurate information about you.

When you get a copy of your personal report, determine the status of your credit file. Study the information in it very well and attempt to remove all unfavorable information in it. All your credit history may not be contained in one file from a firm. So if possible get from other firms too. Some information may be duplicated, or not included in the other file.

You need to note of your full name, social security number, current and previous addresses, spouse's name, and date of birth and make sure that they are correct because they are points used in identifying you. Also, make sure that merchants name, credit account number, date opened, date closed, high credit limit, highest amount of credit used, and repayment history are correct, current and accurate.

After studying the file carefully if you notice any error, write out exact error and the way you think it should be listed. You will find a space on the right-hand side of your report where you may protest any item in your report that you feel incorrect. You will have to attach photocopies along with pertinent information to proof your claim and send it to bureau by mail. When the bureau gets your message they will investigate and send you result of their investigation. You will have to exercise patience during this period because it may take bureau some time to complete their investigation.

The fact that the agency that compiles or can compile information about you is not one will make it almost impossible for you not to encounter problem in future. When you apply for credit in bank, stores or any lending company you may be denied. This does not mean the agency you filed errors on your reports with haven't make changes, it's likely that the bank or store you are trying to deal with have another report about you, possibly from another agency.

So anytime that you are denied credit, you have the right to know why you were turned down! If the bank or stores used a credit report agency, they must provide you with the name and address of the agency that supplied them with the report.

Once you have the contact information of the agency involved, you should make an appointment to visit the credit agency, so that you can review your report, find out information that is causing you to be denied credit, and make corrections if you have enough evidence to proof.

When you are visiting the agency make sure that you present yourself very well. You must dress modestly as your appearance will surely tell the agency staff more about you. If possible take a friend along with you to be a witness to whatever it's said. You have to be very careful when you get to be bureau, don't let the representative of the credit bureau confuse you with unnecessary terms or even upset you in any way. If there is anything you don't understand, ask to have it explained again.

Don't be afraid to demand explanation where you feel the agency is wrong. If there is any information in the report that is not true, point it out, and have it investigated by the agency. Once the agency correct the error you have right to demand that the bureau send correct copies of your report to all creditors who have received the incorrect reports before.

CHAPTER SIX

Credit Repair Company: - a blessing or a course.

Credit repair companies are businesses outfits that offers debit consolidation loans, debt counseling, or debt reorganization plans that guaranteed to stop creditor's collection effort. One thing you have to know is that these companies are established to also make money so you need to be very careful when dealing with this people.

Though, if you are having trouble paying your bills, you may be tempted to turn to one of this companies that claims to offer assistance in solving your problem. Before you sign up with any of credit Repair Company you have to investigate them thoroughly. You have to really understand the services the business provides and what it will cost you before signing up with them. Make sure they have a written contract in place as well.

Most often the consumers that engage the services of most of this business do end up getting more problems. So it's very important that you check office of Better Business Bureau to be sure the company is not in problem already. If there has been a complaint about this company its better you do away with them.

Businesses offering credit repair services may charge substantial fees or a percentage of your debts and fail to deliver. Apart from that their fee will even add up to your debt making it more difficult for consumer to get out of debt. Though it's through that debt problem can be distressing, but you have to be careful when selecting a solution. Some solution providers don't do other things to add to your problem.

CHAPTER SEVEN

Absolute truth about credit repair companies

Despite the fact that U.S Government make it very clear that nobody can repair your credit except you, the credit repair companies keeps growing in number very blessed day. They will promise you heaven and earth just for you to buy their service.

One very important thing most people that are still taking the service of the credit repair companies don't understand is that government's advices are often based on advices of experts. They charge upfront fees, maintenance fees, and monthly fees, all of which you are supposed to place in a trust account.

Why should you in first place pay somebody to help you fix your credit, when it's obvious that most of their results are often temporary? You will end up losing more money.

When you use the service of credit repair companies to fix your bad credit you will be forced to share your personal information with them before they can do anything about your credit. The meaning is that you are liable to identity theft and unwanted mailings you did not solicit for from other companies trying to sell you something.

The whole truth is that you can do what most of these companies do, if you care to know how to do it. All most of them do is to write letters to credit bureaus, listing few information that are false in your credit report. When credit bureau get the information from repair company the will start investigating it.

They will remove the information temporarily during this period, thus giving you clean credit report. Since this report is temporary, if credit bureaus are able to proof their previous action right they will add it back to your report again. So if all you need is a temporary clean credit report, why not do it yourself instead of paying somebody to do it for you. It's obvious, nobody remove negative information that's accurate from your credit report.

Since you have legal right to obtain and dispute a copy of your credit report if there is any error in it, you can improve your credit more effectively on your own.

CHAPTER EIGHT

Credit cards: - types and what you need to know about them.

Nowadays, everybody wants to have at least a credit card. Everywhere you go you see adverts from various banks and other financial institution offering you credit card. However, before you apply for a credit card, there are several factors you need to consider. So it's very important that you know more about the types of cards available, and one that will work best for you.

Secured credit card: - Secured credit cards are types of card that requires a security deposit as collateral before you can get approval. Its type of card that best suit the need of people with no or poor credit who are trying to build their credit history. Your collateral must be equal or greater in value of the credit amount you are applying for.

It can be anything of high monetary value like boat, jewelry, shares, house etc. Just like any other cards, you have to make sure that you study the terms and conditions associated with this card very well before taking the card. It's even very important in this case when you are building your credit history.

Business credit cards: - These are the card that's available for business owners, directors and business executives. They come with several features just like any traditional credit cards. You have to consider the terms and condition for these types of cards too before applying.

Student credit cards are another type of credit card specifically for students. These types of cards are made for students because of their lack of credit history, and if given chance they can build their credit history with such card.

Prepaid credit cards are set of cards that are just acceptable wherever the traditional credit cards are acceptable, but they are not credit card. You will have to always transfer money to your card before you can make use of the card and you may not be able to spend more than you prepaid for the card.

Presently this is almost the best card for people that want to avoid interest and other fees charged on traditional credit card. However, other little charges like monthly fees, application, overlimit and ATM fees are still applicable.

Whichever card you decide to choose make sure that you go over the terms applicable very well to avoid putting yourself in financial bondage. In second part of this article we will continue looking at other types of credit card.

Balance credit cards are unsecured standard cards designed to allow consumers to save money in interest charges by transferring higher interest credit card balance onto a lower interest rate credit card.

Low interest credit cards are other types of non secured standard credit card. They offer either low introductory APR that change to a higher rate after a certain period of time or a low fixed rate. You can take advantage of the low introductory APRs to make larger purchases for now and pay them off several months later.

Air Mile Credit cards are cards that are good for people that travel frequently or planning to go on vacation. It's a form of reward card that allow you opportunity of obtaining a free airline ticket. You will need to accumulate specified air miles before you can be entitled to free ticket. All accumulated mile points will be based on dollar amount of your credit card purchases over a period of time based on predetermined point level.

Specialty credit cards are other set of standard non-secure cards designed specifically for individual business users and students with unique and special needs.

Make sure that you study the terms of any of the card that you pick very well to avoid risking your credit rating. Also, when you pick any of the reward cards make sure you study the forms and offers very well because credit card issuing companies do offer different reward programs and their promotional offers often change. So make sure you thoroughly look over the card's terms and conditions of each specific card before applying.

CHAPTER NINE

Shopping for new Credit Card: - Important tips to consider.

When you are ready to take a new credit card there are lots of factors you need to consider. Among these factors is a credit card term. You need to choose the plan terms that best fit and suit your financial needs. You need to consider plan terms like free period or grace period, annual percentage rate (APR), annual membership or participation fee, transaction fee among others.

It's very important that you understand each of the credit card plan terms before you accept the card to avoid putting yourself in financial bondage. For example if your issuing company did not give free period and you are unable to pay on time your account will be charged and it will ends up adding to your debt.

There are several cases of card theft in recent days so it's advisable that you keep your card very well to avoid unauthorized use. Also don't give away your card information where you aren't feeling secure. Another way to avoid lost or unauthorized use of your card is to only carry the card you think you will use. And in case of lost of your card you need to call issuer and inform them of the lost quickly. So keeping separate records of each of your account number, expiration date and issuer contact information is very important as well.

It's very important that you reconciliate your account when you get statement of account from your card issuer. In other to reconcile your account successfully you need to keep record of receipts where possible and personal note where you don't have receipt. Most likely you will discover errors which could have been added to your statement without you noticing it.

Keeping the above tips in mind will help you while shopping for new card and using it as well.

CHAPTER TEN

Do's and don't of credit card game.

Credit card companies are established to make money from the service they are rendering for their customers. Though they are always happy if their clients have good credit rating, but they are not always happy when you pay off their credit card balance each month. Their wish is that you always carry balance every month so that they can charge interest on your account. Because of this reason they are responding by becoming more creative at finding ways to make money off you.

So there is need for you to be a smart customer so that you did not fall victim as it can end up affecting your credit rating. In this article we will look at few ways you can escape their financial trap.

Make sure you read information you get from your card issuing company. Read every form you get from potential card company. Also, make sure you study the bill and every other information you get from your credit card company over time because they can change their terms of your card agreement with as little as 15 days. And if you are careless to take note of this it may end up affecting your credit.

Make sure you avoid late payment of your fees. If you make late payment you can be subjected to larger balance on your account and your card issuing company may hike your interest rate as a result of this.

Avoid carrying balance every month because you will end up paying far more than you should for everything you charge to your card. Make sure you pay for everything your charge within the grace period, if there is any and you will not fall victim of high interest rate. Failure to do this will lead to accumulation of debt, which will end up spoiling your credit report if you are not careful.

If you are not feeling comfortable with the service you are getting from your issuing company or any of their terms – make sure you complaint. Don't die in silence. Because of the competition most of this companies are facing they will be forced to answer your complaint, and as a matter of fact make adjustment where possible. For example if you've been getting high interest fee you can have it lowered by just making your request to your issuing company.

You are free to shop around when you are thinking of

getting a new card. Why should you be forced to one company you don't feel you are comfortable with when there are lots of them out there. Shop around – you can get whatever you want.

You can get interest rate you want, grace period or even a card without annual fee charge. So go out there, compare the rates, and terms of several cards before you make your choice. The choice you make today will surely determine your credit report tomorrow somehow.

Most card holders are careless when it comes to checking their credit report with the credit bureau or agencies involved. If you pay your balance on time and don't carry balance often you have to make sure that your card issuing company reports your performance to bureau on time. You may possibly want to get loan in future and your present credit performance will help you a lot in getting approval on time.

Bad spending habit is one of the viruses that have infected most of card users in recent years. As a matter of fact, use of internet has even made it easy for every card user to get anything they want within minutes. So may find it impossible to control their spending. Most of the website even makes it so easy that you will not even know when you are giving them your card information.

There is a way out – make sure that you keep your card away most of the time. Most especially when you are accessing internet and when you are going out. If it's a must that you carry card because of emergencies, take only one along. However, you can reduce or even stop the bad spending virus if you stop buying things on impulse. If you are to buy anything at all make plan for it in advance.

CHAPTER ELEVEN

How to get credit card of your choice.

It's very easy to get a new major credit card of your choice these days. The most important thing has always been the state of your credit rating. Since your credit will be rated on your relationship with lending companies and banks, it's very possible for you to improve or even build up your credit ratings with banks.

If you make sure that once you get loan you always make payments by the agreed time, sooner, you can move to another credit procurement program like getting Visa or Master card from all major banks you've borrowed from. These will be possible for you because they already know more about your credit rating.

As a matter of fact they have record of your transactions with them. Once you are able to get card from these banks you've been dealing with before, it will be easy for you to get credit card from any other banks that provides same service.

What most people that are dying to get new credit cards don't know is that most of these banks are also looking for new customers. They are always ready to do everything legitimate to get you because they know they will profit from you. That is why most of them offer preferential interest rate. Providing that you have kept to your repayment agreements on all loans and cards, there is no reason why you should be refused any cards for which you apply.

Once you've achieve good credit rating, credit card companies, banks, and other lending companies will see you as a good risk. Thus, you will find it easy to get card from them anytime. Also you will be surprise at series of offers you will be getting from several other credit card companies that will also want you to have card from them.

They will trust you because they must have got every detail of your credit rating from your former bank. That exactly is the main reason why building your credit rating from scratch is very important.

CHAPTER TWELVE

Buy Now Pay Later – Disadvantages of using credit card and how to get over it.

Credit cards offer you so many advantages. With credit card you can purchase several things you need to make yourself more comfortable. But despite all the advantages that comes with holding a credit card it can create a lot of problems for you if you are not careful.

It create a lot of problems for some people if you are not careful you can end up incurring high finance and interest charges that will make it almost impossible to repay back your bill and thus, lead you to huge credit card debt you may never get out. However, it's possible for you to stay clear of debt if you can follow few tips provided in this article and that of your finance consultant.

Consulting your financial advisor is very important when you are thinking of applying for credit card. You can both reason together on your financial needs.

When you get the card make sure you keep every receipts and compare them with your monthly bill, there may be discrepancies which can drown you in debt if you don't discover it. Once you discover any, report to your credit card company immediately.

Giving your credit card to friends and family is one of the ways to incure more debt. So keep your credit card away from friends, families and strangers.

Make sure you don't owe than you can repay at the end of the month as it can damage your credit and hurt your chances of getting credit in future. See credit card as loan you have to pay back. You can avoid this by paying your bill on time, if possible, pay it every month.

One of the mistake most card holders makes is paying of one credit card with another. It's a complete bad habit. It will surely lead you to more debt, and you may find it difficult to get out of it.

CHAPTER THIRTEEN

How to avoid high interest charges on your credit card.

There is a credit term call grace period – it's a period within which you may pay your bill without being charged interest. It's usually a period of 25-30days before interest kicks in. Recently, most issuing companies are eliminating this grace period and instead offering a low fixed interest rate. The question now is – which one is better between grace period and low fixed interest rate?

It will be a bit difficult to have one answer that will favour everybody. Some prefer paying their bills in full within the normal grace period. To this group of people the grace period will be better. It will be advisable for them to shop for grace period cards and avoid no-grace-period cards.

Some banks do charge interest from the day they process your charge slip when you use your card to get cash. If you normally pay your bill in full you still need to shop for card that offers very low interest rate plus grace period, if you are to avoid interest charges on your account. However, for those that usually carry a balance each month, the low interest rate will be good for them. If you are in this group you can even shop for institutions that periodically offer cards with no fee for the first year.

Most issuing company often offers "premium" credit cards such as "goldcards" and Premier VISA. They are fancy cards that come with travel insurance benefit and extra protection when your card is lost or stolen. These institutions will rarely use the highly annual service fees which you will be subjected to as their marketing point. So it's advisable to beware of these cards. There is no reason for paying such high service fees. As a matter of fact it did not really worth it if you can have a lower interest or grace period card.

CHAPTER FOURTEEN

How to get loan even if you have bad credit.

Nowadays, lots of people depends on loan, or other form of credit to acquire new car, pay off bills, finance home improvements, pay for long awaited vacation, consolidate debt, and other important things. Before you can get loan from bank, they will have to consider your credit rating.

In the past, if you have bad credit you may find it difficult to get loan most especially secure personal loans. However, it's now possible for people with bad credit to obtain loan from banks and other financial institution with ease.

Most banks have realized that bad credit can happen to anybody. They believe that it's possible to improve your credit score or totally change your bad credit, thus they prefer giving second chance to people with bad credit to give them the opportunity to proof their abilities. This type of loan is called bad credit loan.

Bad credit loan provides people with credit problem to improve or create a completely new credit history by starting afresh. With bad credit loan you can get the money you need. If you repaid the money to the bank as agreed, it will make it easier for you to get more credit in future and you will be building new credit score in the process.

Banks that offers bad credit loan often have different plans. Some will request for high value properties like car, real estate as collateral before they can lend you money. They often asked for this because of possibility that you may default on your loan based on your bad credit rating they have.

It's going to be easy for them to get their money back by selling your property you offer as collateral if you default on your loan. Other banks may approve bad credit loan without collateral but they may charge you higher interest rate. They are allowed by financial regulators to charge you more interest than regular banks can charge on normal loan because not all banks can afford granting such substandard loans.

If you still find it difficult to get bank that will grant your loan application, I will advice that you consider applying for a secured loan or reduce amount you are requesting for. You can get loan with or without good credit score. If you shop around you will see different lenders that can grant your offer. You just have to make sure that you repaid loan bank on time to avoid having your credit blacklisted completely.

CHAPTER FIFTEEN

Important Credit Card Plan terms you must consider.

Credit card companies keeps pushing hard to get more customers daily by giving "pre-approved" card offers to would be clients through mail. Chances are you've gotten one of this offers in your mail in recent days. Such promotion has being in existences long before now. Though getting such card is good to some extent and getting one will be helpful however, you don't have to rush into getting one without considering the plan terms associated very well.

There are lots of plan terms that you really need to study very well while shopping for credit card if you are not ready to put yourself in financial prison. These terms affect your overall cost. In this article we will take a look at some of this credit card plan terms you need to consider before choosing a company to deal with. Get a cup of coffee while we discuss each of terms you need to consider.

Reward program is term used for marketing strategies used by most banks or issuing banks to get more customers. They designed additional incentives to convince clients to get card from them. There are several types of rewards programs. Most common are free airline miles, cash back from purchases, and instant discounts.

Consider a company that gives **"free period"** or grace period over others. Because without free period, the card issuer may impose finance charge from the date you use your card or from the date each transaction is posted to your account. Free period allow you to pay back your balance in full before due date in other to avoid finance charges and it's usually mail at least 14 days before the due date, giving you enough time to pay.

Periodic rate of a credit card is another term you have to know about. This is the amount of interest that is charged for a single period of the year. It can fluctuate from month to month.

Another very important term to take note of is **APR (Annual Percentage Rate)** which is the measure of the cost of credit, expressed as a yearly rate. APR often changes when there is a change in interest rates or other economic indicators. Still companies must disclose this before you open the account and on your account statements.

Preset Credit Limits: some card issuing companies have a preset credit limits on their cards. Receiver can not be able to exceed this credit limit because the issuing company will decline the transaction above limit they place on the card.

Apart from the annual percentage rate, you need to consider how much the issuer's charges for membership fee. The annual membership or participation fees varies, it's often between $25 and $100.

You also need to know about method issuers will use in calculating your finance charge if you don't have a free period, or if you are expected to pay for purchases over time. Knowing this will help you keep your finance charge low by measuring your buying patterns and paying back on time.

BONUS SECTION

Recession Proofing Your Job

The first thing you want to do is protect your job. As I mentioned earlier, it's going to be the small start-up companies who haven't firmly embedded themselves into society that will feel the ax the fastest when a recession comes around. When people stop spending money, they're going to be among the first companies to stop receiving it because they simply haven't had time to dig in their roots.

If you work for a company that's going to feel very little effects as a result of a recession you have very little to worry about. Regardless of what company you work for, however, now is a great time to start making yourself indispensible. It's simple fact that the employees that are the first to go when a company starts making lay-offs are the ones who aren't deemed to be important enough to stay-sort of like acceptable loss in a war zone. Those employees have to go in order for the company to thrive.

Making yourself an indispensible part of your company is the first step toward recession proofing your job. Even companies that are cutting down on their staff are going to hesitate to get rid of individuals who are essential to their company's daily operations. This would be an excellent time to consider volunteering to take on extra work or become more actively involved in long term projects or contracts.

If you can, involve yourself in several projects your company is working on (obviously without stretching yourself so thin that you can no longer do your job to the best of your ability). The more pies you have your fingers in, the more hesitant management will be to let you go. In times of recession companies may be cutting back on their employees, but that doesn't mean that they're going to be able to cut back on the amount of work they have to do. It just means that that work is going to be re-delegated. If you're already actively involved in several ongoing projects the company will find it much easier to simply accord you extra responsibilities on these projects than to attempt to bring a new man up to speed.

A heads up-this is NOT the time to attempt to apply for a promotion or a transfer, however promising that transfer may be. The minute you accept this type of move you become the new man on the block, and immediately become more vulnerable when the time comes to go through and decide who will go and who will stay. Right before the string of layoffs in 2007 due to the termination of numerous government contracts one well known government agency had just opened a new department and moved a large quantity of their oldest and most experienced employees on over. Despite the fact that many of these employees had put in more time with the company than the management they were working under, because their department was "new" they were among the first to lose their jobs when the company started laying off.

Attitude counts-a LOT. A recent article published by Fortune magazine stated that when management is trying to decide who will stay and who will go, often attitude and the employee's ability to boost morale is as strong a determining factor as their ability to do their job. When the going gets tough, the tough have to get going. Remember, companies trying to stay on top during a recession are going to have higher expectations of their employees than ever before. The only way these employees are going to be able to meet those expectations is if they are able to keep their morale high.

An employee who drags that morale down is going to quickly find themselves looking for another job.

Just in Case...

Hopefully the economic recession isn't going to impact your job-but that doesn't mean you shouldn't take precautions. You don't want to wait until you're holding your pink slip in hand and wondering how you're going to make next month's mortgage payment to start looking around for another job, and you don't want to wait until you need something from them to touch base with your old bosses and co-workers and your friends and acquaintances that might be able to offer you work when the going gets rough.

Network

It's all about networking. If you know anything about real estate you know "location, location, location" is every agent's mantra. (Right after "Buy low and sell high".) A piece of property that's within easy walking distance to schools, grocery stores and public transportation is going to be far more desirable than one that is miles away from everything, no matter how beautiful the location.

The same thing applies to you when the time comes for you to find a job. That house in the middle of everything is going to sell much more quickly, and you, in the middle of a huge network of friends and potential employers, are going to be able to find work much more rapidly. If you've kept in touch with your bosses and associates, both past and present, you'll not only probably already know who's hiring and who's not, you may have the inside track when it comes to finding another job.

If you wait to get in touch with them until you've been laid off, however, you're going to find yourself struggling. They're going to know that the only reason you're contacting them is because you're hoping to get a job, and they're going to look at you unfavorably-not only because you're willing to use your friends that way in the first place, but that you would be caught so unprepared. They're going to be far more concerned with their own affairs at that point than they are about yours.

Be Visible

No matter how much you've been looking forward to spending the next three weeks onboard a Carnival cruise ship, when your company starts making budget cuts is absolutely, positively not the time to take an extended vacation. You can't show someone how valuable you are if you're not there! When they sit down to review employee records and someone asks, "Hey, where's...?" and someone else answers, "Oh, he's on vacation..."- well, you can imagine where that conversation is going to go.

That doesn't mean you have to deprive yourself of a well earned week away from the office. If you tend to take your vacations in bulk (disappearing for two to three weeks at a time) this is a fine opportunity to spread those vacations out a little-a week here, three or four days there will give you a break while still keeping you in the corporate eye. No one expects you to work yourself to death (and if they do, they'll never admit it in public). You just don't want to take that vacation at a time when taking a little break could turn into an extended one-as in, permanently.

Remember, the average recession in the United States only lasts eleven months. Giving up your extended vacation for a single year is a small price to pay for keeping your job...and your paycheck...and your 401K...and your health insurance...You get the picture. You can always enjoy that month in Aruba next year.

Offer Suggestions on Ways to Save the Company Money

In the middle of a recession even companies that have historically been very employee oriented are going to have to shift their focus from creating a great place to work to creating a way to trim the fat off of their budget while continuing to remain competitive in the marketplace and lure in consumers who would otherwise prefer to spend their money elsewhere. This is going to be their top priority!

Because saving money while still continuing to make money is going to be a vital part of the company's continued existence (and because it can be so difficult to do in an economy that thrives on the idea that you have to spend money to make money) an employee that can help them achieve that goal is going to instantly become one of the company's greatest assets. You don't dispose of assets that are generating a tangible return in the middle of a recession. Employees that can help a company move forward while at the same time preserving their bottom line are going to be worth their weight in gold in the eyes of the corporate bigwigs, and you can guarantee that these individuals are not going to be the ones standing in the unemployment line!

Can't come up with any clever suggestions to help your company cut its costs? Here's some ideas to get you started:

Trim the fat on the office supplies. You'd be amazed at what the average office spends in pencils, paper and folders a month!

Find a way to go through and lower

production costs without losing quality.

If you can discover a way to decrease the cost of transporting your products you will instantly become your office's golden child! The increase in the cost of oil (and subsequently gasoline) has spurred an almost ludicrous increase in the cost of transporting goods, which in turn has forced companies to raise the price of their goods, which in turn is leading to the loss of business in the recessed economy as customers complain about the increase in the price of goods and take their business elsewhere.

New employee perks. Companies that don't offer their employees any perks whatsoever usually don't have employees for very long. Even the most unconcerned companies generally host a Christmas party or other annual event for the people that keep the wheels of their company turning, as well as a steady stream of incentives throughout the year to keep morale high and encourage greater productivity. If you can think of a steady stream of employee (and client) perks that will require the company to part with less money out of pocket you will be well on your way to establishing yourself as an invaluable member of your company's team.

Keep Your Skills Up to Date

It doesn't matter what industry you happen to be in, sweeping changes in supply, demand and technology are going to require you to stay up to date with what's happening in the field. If you've simply coasted along up until this point, grandfathering your way along while your co-workers went back to school, attended certification classes and furthered their education, you're going to find yourself in a sticky situation in the middle of a recession.

When preparing to weather a recession companies are going to consider the long term outlook for their company rather than the short term, which means that their priority when considering which employees are going to go and which ones are going to stay is finding high quality workers that are going to be able to help the company keep pushing forward in changing times.

This is one of those times when that insignificant little piece of paper helps.

Unless you have worked extensively with the technologies or programs that your company specializes in and know it inside, outside and backwards without the benefit of taking a class or two to show you how to do it, you're going to find yourself pushed out of the way in favor of a younger employee who has taken the time to expand their horizons.

Education counts. If you haven't already, take this opportunity to see what kind of tuition reimbursement your company offers and what certifications are available in your field.

THERE IS NO POSSIBLE WAY TAKING THIS STEP WILL HURT YOU!

Ideally, furthering your education will make your boss

see what a valuable asset you are to your company and keep your job secure during these trying times; however, if your company still decides to let you go these certifications are going to look great on a resume when you go to find another job. Companies love ambitious, motivated employees as much as they love well educated, experienced ones, and by taking the initiative and obtaining these certifications without any nudging from your boss you'll be proving yourself to be both.

Keep Looking

Walking around advertising the fact that you're looking for another job never endears you to employers, but covertly doing so in the face of an economic recession and a possible lay-off is just good sense. By continuing to job hunt even though you already have a job you'll be accomplishing several things:

First and foremost, you'll be able to keep a weather eye on what's coming available on the market-and with whom. Although you don't want to be the new kid on the block when companies are looking to start cutting their payroll, if a favorable position becomes available with a company that stands a very good chance of weathering a recession while your company is almost guaranteed to cut your job in the next eight to twelve weeks, you'd be a fool not to snatch at the opportunity.

It might mean taking a little bit of a chance, but the bottom line is that by doing so you'll also be setting yourself up to be gainfully employed while your co-workers are standing in the unemployment line.

Secondly, you'll be preparing yourself for change. If you've ever seen the children's video Kung Fu Panda you'll remember the infamous words of the immortal Master Oogway-"There is no good news or bad news. There is only news." The determining factor in whether news is viewed as good or bad is precisely that-how you view it.

If you look at a recession and a possible layoff as a stimulus for change (change that you can be prepared for if you make the effort) then you will have no problem when it comes time to say goodbye to the old and hello to the new. On the other hand, if you're still rooted in the thought that the world is going to come to an end if you lose your job and have to go hunting for another one you're going to find yourself mired in confusion and misery when you're handed that pink slip-a mucky place that is going to hold on to you until the consequences become all too obvious.